With love for my granddaughter Sophia—may your eyes always be fixed on Jesus.

–C.C.M.

"If we confess our sins, he is faithful and just, and will forgive our sins and cleanse us from all unrighteousness."

–1 John 1:9

In accordance with CIC 827, permission to publish has been granted on September 12, 2022, by the Most Reverend Mark S. Rivituso, Auxiliary Bishop, Archdiocese of St. Louis. Permission to publish is an indication that nothing contrary to Church teaching is contained in this particular work. It does not imply any endorsement of the opinions expressed in the publication, or a general endorsement of any author: nor is any liability assumed by this permission.

Text copyright © 2023 by Claudia Cangilla McAdam. All rights reserved.

Published by Ascension Publishing Group, LLC.

With the exception of short excerpts used in articles and critical reviews, no part of this work may be reproduced, transmitted, or stored in any form whatsoever, printed or electronic, without the prior written permission of the publisher.

Ascension
PO Box 1990
West Chester, PA 19380
1-800-376-0520
ascensionpress.com

Cover design by: Lily Fitzgibbons

Printed in the United States of America
22 23 24 25 26 5 4 3 2 1

ISBN 978-1-954881-81-5

A Miracle for Micah

Written by CLAUDIA CANGILLA McADAM
Illustrated by GINA CAPALDI

West Chester, Pennsylvania

Micah watched the house where the fisherman Peter lived.
All seemed quiet on this Sabbath morning.
Everyone was at the synagogue.

The boy crept up the stone stairway to the roof. He silently tiptoed to a large basket and lifted the lid. Layers of fish lay packed in salt. His empty stomach rumbled. A couple more days, and the fish would be completely dried. He could just help himself to them then!

Someone coughed in the house below. Micah froze. Soundlessly, he dug a finger into the mud-covered straw that thatched the roof. He pressed his eye against the opening.

It was an old lady, sick and in bed. She had not gone to the synagogue. Micah needed to leave before the others returned.

Too late! Peter and his brother Andrew came in. Jesus was there, too.

"Her fever is high," murmured Peter. Micah saw sadness stamped on his face. The woman was dying.

Jesus sat on the side of the bed. He took the woman's hand and lifted her up. She was well!

"You all must be hungry," she said, rising to feed them.

Micah forgot about his own hunger.

He couldn't stop staring through the hole in the straw. How had a woman near death been cured? He wished he could keep watching, but he didn't want to be found near the fish. He noiselessly left Peter's roof, wondering at what he had seen.

Three days later, Micah brought his brother Joel. They hid behind the wall of the house and waited. The men were gone. Finally, the old woman walked out of the door and down to the seaside, where she sat mending nets.

"Why are we here?" Joel whispered.

"To get fish," Micah answered.

"But this is not the market!"

Micah pressed his finger to his lips. "It's better!"

Up the stone steps he scampered. He swiftly snatched some dried fish from the basket. Soon, he was back at Joel's side.

"You stole those!" Joel cried. "Mama gave you a coin to buy them."

"I have a better use for that money," Micah said.

At the market, Micah did something he never had enough money to do. He bought two raisin cakes sweetened with honey and offered one to his brother.

Joel stared at him, sad at what he had seen.

The next week, Micah left their village early, before Joel was awake.

At Peter's house, people were everywhere. They jammed into the doorway. They crowded around the window. They perched on tree branches.

There was no way Micah could steal fish. He could hear Jesus preaching inside.

Four people carried a man on a mat. "Let us in, please," one of them begged. "Our friend cannot walk.
We know Jesus can heal him."

They could not squeeze through the front door.
Micah had an idea.

"Come this way," he said, leading them up the stone staircase.
He showed them how to open the straw on the roof.

When they lowered their friend down, no one would be paying any attention to Micah. He could get more fish!

But Micah couldn't take his eyes off Jesus.

"Your sins are forgiven," Jesus told the paralyzed man Then he said, "Rise, take up your bed and go home."

Micah was amazed by what he had seen.

When everyone left, Micah snatched some fish
and crept down the staircase. He stopped when
he locked eyes with Jesus standing at the bottom.

Jesus touched the fish Micah carried.
"What would Joel say if he saw those?"

Micah stuck out his jaw. "He won't."
Micah had left his brother behind for a reason.

Jesus smiled sadly. He motioned to a boy in the shadows. It was Joel!

Micah's face burned with shame.

Jesus placed his hand on Joel's head and looked at Micah.

"Not only have your actions hurt me. You took something that belonged to Peter. And what example have you given your brother? What kind of person are you becoming, Micah?" Jesus asked.

Jesus' words felt like a heavy weight on the boy's heart. He looked down at the fish. Did he care more about them than he did about Joel ... and Peter ... and Jesus?
Hot tears spilled down Micah's cheeks. He fell to his knees.

"I'm sorry," he said, holding out what he had stolen.

"Forgive me, Lord."

Jesus embraced him. "Your sins are forgiven. Go, and sin no more."

Micah ran back to the roof and replaced the fish.

His brother grinned at what he had seen.

The next time his mother sent him to the market, Micah brought Joel. As they walked past the woman selling raisin cakes, Micah's stomach growled. But he took Joel's hand and marched past the stand.

Micah purchased five loaves of barley bread, the food of the poor. There was only enough money for two fish, and he added them to his basket.

The hill they climbed on their way home was covered with people. Jesus stood teaching them.

Micah inched nearer.

"The people are hungry," he heard a man tell Jesus.

"Where shall we buy bread for all of them to eat?" Jesus asked.

"We could work for half a year and not have enough money to buy bread for everyone," the man answered.

Micah spotted Andrew nearby. "Jesus can have these," he said, lifting his basket

Andrew showed the bread and fish to Jesus. "This won't go far," Andrew said.

Jesus smiled his thanks and took Micah's offering. Micah tingled with excitement as he pulled Joel down to sit on the grass.

"But what will mama say when you come home with no food?" Joel asked his brother.

Jesus whispered to the boys, "She'll say, 'Well done, good and faithful servant.'"

He bent over the bread and blessed and broke it.

Micah's eyes never left the Lord. He couldn't wait to see what Jesus would do next.

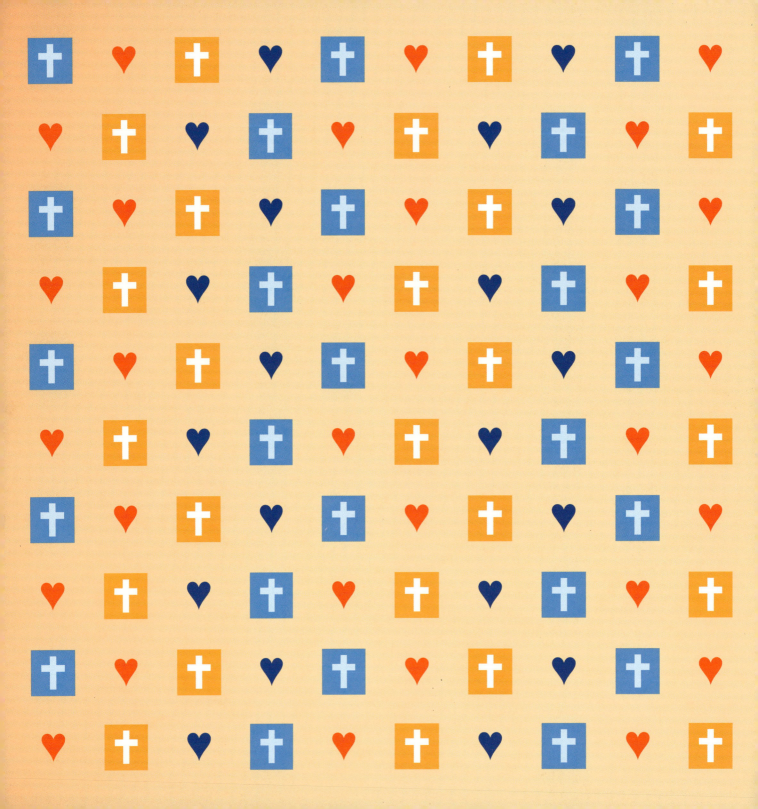